Looking for you

Peter Phillips

HEARING EYE

Published by Hearing Eye
Box 1, 99 Torriano Avenue, London NW5 2RX

ISBN: 1 870841 816

This publication has been made possible with the
financial assistance of London Arts.

Printed by Catford Print Centre
Typeset by Daniel James at mondo designo

*In memory of Linda Phillips
and for my family*

Acknowledgements

Some of these poems, or versions of them, first
appeared in: The Affectionate Punch, Between The
Lines, Brando's Hat, Envoi, The Express, Frayed At
The Edges (Hearing Eye 1997), The Frogmore
Papers, Orbis, Other Poetry, Poetry London, Poetry
Nottingham International, Poetry On The Buses
1997 and 1998, Poetry Street N16, Seam, Smith
Knoll, Staple New Writing, Weyfarers, Work
Anthology (Katabasis), A London Anthology
(Enitharmon).

'Pear Tree' and a version of 'Fog' were performed in
March 2001 at the Queen Elizabeth Hall as part of a
new song cycle celebrating the seventy-fifth
birthday of Hans Werner Henze.

CONTENTS

Looking For You

Looking At Us

Closeness

Reflections

Night Tales

London Poems

Fox Tales

Poems Have No Stamina

LOOKING FOR YOU

GRANDFATHER

I was too busy being young, drinking milkshakes,
having train rides on the seafront
to ask any questions.
If he were here, I would hold his hand,
ask why he always wore suits,
who passed him the worry gene
I took from mother like a baton.

I didn't know him long enough, not nearly.
One moment he was driving us around Southsea,
going slow in the fast lane,
being told by grandmother to indicate properly;
then he was mother's father,
being talked about a lot
and I asked why the nursing home had let him out at night.

FOG

When father died he must have known
you were already leaving us.
He would have seen you fumble in your bag,
write your day on a scrap of paper
then fuss when you lost it.

But Mother, we all make lists,
so when you stopped,
it was then—when I saw them lying
on the dining table, little pieces of memory
waiting to be picked up—I wondered.

It was almost timeless, the slow movement
from here to a strangeness so slight
outsiders would not have noticed.
But when you talked of fog, I knew it had happened
and with it came your war with tears,
father's death, and the feeling of difference,
hoping you were wrong.

SECOND CHILDHOOD

It happened in the night, Mother.
Sky, black as the dread
you saw in your sisters' eyes,
dropped black dots,
sprinkled you with childhood,
the same second coming they suffered.

I know you find it difficult to explain.
It's like wanting to tell me something
and then it's gone, or half there
and when you say it, it comes out
as something else, but not all the time.

When the hairdresser asks
'What are you doing this weekend?'
how will you answer?

Do not think too long
or your tongue, tired and tangled,
will sieve the words.
Just answer, 'Nothing special,'
or smile at the hairdresser, Mother.
You can get away with a smile.

REGENT'S PARK

After forty years the boating pond is smaller.
Here I tried to drown my fear,
a boulder in my chest
as I circled to escape Victoria Station,
the train journey to boarding school,
a last holiday treat from mother.

Now mother's treat is the rose garden.
Her face likes the stroke of the scented breeze.
She shuffles to the ducks, licks an ice cream,
on holiday from herself,
escapes from sitting inside her head.

Nearby a swan treads water, searches
for her young, splashes down;
they ride the surf to her wing.

AT THE PSYCHIATRIST

How many heads has this man visited?
I like his quiet dishevelment;
he seems to know the place where mother has gone
and when he asks her where she is,
names of the Queen's children,
who is the Prime Minister —
I'm in there competing.

He offers the latest drugs,
their list of side effects so ill
I begin to waiver. When mother is asked
if she'll take them, she agrees,
but already the line between consent
and what's good for her has blurred.

As we leave she thanks him
and all the time I can hear
her silent fist, beating, beating...

POWER OF ATTORNEY

How do you ask someone
to pass you their life?

The document looks so ordinary.
Folded, stapled in the corner,
not even a piece of ribbon to bind the words.
It seals her history,
her future. From now mother is not
in her hands. That signature
is my trust, my sister's;
it seems a natural thing to hold.

Now I need to think for her,
and when I do it's as if I'd always
done it. Decisions about food, carers,
medication… never to
go across a red or amber light.
Decisions about money, where to live,

and always
there are father's grave words:
'Never put her in a nursing home.'

MOTHER'S FRIEND

A strawberry tart, rye bread
with a well-done crust,
that's what I wanted.
But into the bakers came mother's friend,
walked towards me, taking ten steps back.

His words didn't mingle with the Danish,
Madeira or chocolate cake. They flew
at me, straight past the new bread —
took its breath away — and mine.

I could see the question in his eyes:
'How's mother?
I've been meaning to phone.'
I should have told him
but I didn't want to get into symptoms.
'I'm going to call and see her,' he said.
'What's a good time?'
       'It's best to ring me first,
       She's a bit forgetful.'

He wrote down the invisible number.
As he walked away, the bread breathed out
and the last strawberry tart was sold.

SILENT TONGUE

The nurse is too urgent, too efficient.
She's washing mother's skin away
and she doesn't have any to spare.

Tired from a sit-down shower,
she sits in her chair.
Mother's good at sitting.

The chair wraps round her, holds
mother in a daze.
She has been asking for me,
and later, when I say I'm going,
she says 'thank you'.

If there were more words
she would telephone, but her silent tongue
needs the jolt of a 'goodbye'.

TEA WITH MOTHER

Strong tea. No sugar. That's
what she liked, out of a china cup
with a gold edged lip,
a slow dash of milk
and a chat.

Today she drinks from a plastic mug
with a lid, sips it slowly.

Outside the London plane trees are tired.
I can see them sagging.

WHITE BLOSSOM

Yesterday, when I said hello,
you smiled your son smile
and for an instant you were mother.
Today I'm waving to you,
looking close into your distant eyes
level with your thoughts. What are they?
Why can't I break through?

White blossom is breaking open.
Set against the sky and painted stucco of houses
it lights my street.

Tomorrow I'll become an expert on wheelchairs,
decide whether to rent or buy,
do the calculations.
How long will you use it?

Soon the blossom will stream away
and trees fall into leaf.

PLAYTHING

A bed bath at night and again in the morning
it soothes you, like a piece of chocolate,
photos of grandchildren.

This week your house was sold, black bags
full of you, in piles for Oxfam.
We should be doing this when you're dead,

but death thinks you are a game, a plaything
to be toyed with and like a spoilt child
wants his way, to do things in his time.

I'm getting used to your death, this slowest
of processions. When you're gone there will be
a hole in my head and part of my mind

and daily thoughts will have to think differently.
The trouble is, you have become a habit.

LOOKING FOR YOU

Mother, I feel as if I'm fumbling
through your dressing table, opening
drawers for bits of paper, photos
to touch a private past.
If I hear someone on the stairs,
I'll say I've been looking for you.

I've said all the words you wouldn't say
but thought about as you cared for sister after sister.

Those words are now my language
and as I take them from you, I know
they cannot make you shiver any more.

I hear the wanderings
of your mind, see you drift
between now and earlier times,

and as I sit you in your chair I feel
your thin weight of seventy-five years slipping
lightly from me. 'Beautiful,' you say
when you see a child on TV
and I know you are still here.

I'm a trespasser, have entered
without knocking.
I wanted a memory,
some poetry, but there is none.
I'm closing your bedroom door.

LOOKING AT US

THE UNEXPECTED

It only takes a small thing,
a broken wheelchair,
her fridge not defrosting
or faulty oven, to make
sparks ignite on the tracks on my head.

I try to organise it now; tomorrow
is too late
and there may be something else.
I feel today shunt into the sidings.

I've become used to the unexpected,
can hear the phone dialling
before it rings.

CARING

When I was a schoolboy,
mother might send postal orders
with her letters.
These, a jar of peanut butter, oranges
and her visits kept me happy.

Sometimes I try and undo
the knot of caring:
love, duty, responsibility?

Perhaps it doesn't matter,
so long as we do it.

LOST CONVERSATION

I've never been a great talker,
always felt it a bit overrated
and as for communication,
that's a scientific art.

But it's conversation, the repartee
between my brother and sisters I miss.
There seems no time
for the light stuff, just the weight
of exchanges of information
about the business of caring.

Unfortunately, we've become good at it.

WRONG DIAGNOSIS

My sister doubts mother's diagnosis
but the name will make no difference.

She says mother's jam pastries, apple pies
with enough cream to drown in,
and all that red meat, are to blame.
She tells me to take aspirin.

We both think we will follow mother,
enter her silent storm of a world
where thoughts are a junket of words.
So anything to get the diagnosis wrong.

She may be right, but why, I ask
did those pills the colour of sunlight
untie her tongue, give her
six months with the curtains drawn back?

I ate mother's meals,
still have their taste in my mouth.
Next time a memory makes a mad dash
from my head, sprints into the ether,
I will buy those aspirin.

FATHER

If he were alive,
what would he be thinking?

He'd sit legs crossed, swivel the chair
round when I came into the room.

He was a man who knew the secret
of selling was always in the buying;

who nearly swallowed his teeth
laughing at my jokes;

who surprised mother
with a Concord trip to Iceland;

who tipped the Zoo Keeper
so we could throw cabbages to hippos;

who didn't mind having a dog
so long as he didn't have to walk it;

who always took us to see a pantomime,
and mother to good restaurants.

But I never heard him ask her
if she wanted a cup of tea.

CLOSENESS

POEM FOR MY FIRST WIFE

A candle on the kitchen window sill
commemorates your death.
It burns all night in a small glass,
silhouettes the room as once you did.

SIX YEARS ON

I still clench my foot like a fist,
grind my jaw so the muscles ache.

Ten years tiptoeing to the edge;
I held her hand as she fell.

Don't tell me it was meant
or she had served her time.

Misfortune was her fate.
My guilt is the effect.

PAINFUL PRAYER

Last night I shut my eyes and felt a tear
so hot it singed a blemish on my face
and burnt the pillow with a painful prayer,
a dream of memories that won't erase.

I often feel her hands, a smile and voice
that pull me to her, a kiss which flutters
in my mouth, comforts me with lips as moist
as breath and calms me till nothing matters.

So when I think of prayer, belief and hope,
I do not see bright sunshine fill the sky —
just shades of grey and how she tried to cope
when told she'd never hear a grandchild cry.

And now the moon has disappeared from sight
the morning will be darker than first light.

CLOSENESS

Sometimes my son and daughter hug
each other so tight.

Maybe they miss their mother holding them,
her cheeks as new linen.

Both let go of God, dumped him
as they might a boy or girl friend,
certain of hurt—
joined me.

When I see their closeness, I feel
her first hug while dancing, nerves
on the journey to Bow
and ice of that front room, igloo cold,
then hot kissing to Nana Mouskouri.

I still wonder why she let me kiss her,
me gawky in open sandals,
and on the first date too.

PEAR TREE

As winter chill thawed away, I walked
in the garden. It was, I remember
a Tuesday and I came in and touched your photograph,
the one with the wooden frame,
with you in the garden
and light all around. You
had a smile and the beds were full of colour.

Behind you was a cherry tree
and its pinched buds were still hopeful.
Now it has gone and we have planted
a pear tree in its place.
We did that on a Tuesday as well.

In a few months pears will ripen
and fall. Leaves sodden with autumn rain
will turn to mould as winter frost
starts to bite again.

THE COLOUR BLUE

When you were a colour, were you ever blue?
'Little girl in the blue dress make my day,'
is what I sang beside the lake.
It was our song —
I can hear the words
bright as the summer of your dress.

Where is it now, that cotton dress,
the one your mother made in August blue?
It's far away, gone with words
I sometimes hear towards the end of day,
the tune of a song we sang
sitting on the bank of a lake.

I'd been before, seen black lakes,
dark hills, sky the colour of your dress.
I didn't think I knew that song.
It tripped lightly from the blue
inside my head to close the day,
not as thoughts but words.

Up they climbed those words
in the drizzled air above the lake
and in the early morning hush of day
it rained and drenched your dress.
The sky was full of cloudy blue
and that was when I heard our song.

It was strange to hear the rain and song,
a shower of music pouring words,
a serenade of blue.
And when they scattered on the lake
you rose, took off your dress,
laid it in the heat of day.

There in the middle of the day
in the glare of sun and song
we stayed, and when your dress
was dry we listened to those words,
cooled our faces in the lake
and the sky became a different shade of blue.

I think about that day, the words
of a song beside the lake,
your dress, the colour blue.

INDELIBLE KISS

Don't promise me a cliché,
the one of love and life.
Kiss me inside my head
where I hurt;
cradle my face.
Sign your name in years.
Kiss me indelibly.

DOZEN STONES

Inside my head a dozen stones,
poems of a private time,
grind like trampled pebbles,
elegies composing in my mind.

And who for? Not for her the purging
of a moment's memory printed on the page,
an indulgent recollection honed
like polished stone.

Between the blur of sense and feeling
and the balance of a right decision,
there is an instinct, intuitive with reason —
poems where I cannot go.

If I want her memory as a light
these stones will not be poems.

DRIVE TO ME FROM ROMFORD

Drive to me from Romford
under skies of beer and cloud.
Stay with me in Hampstead, where today the sun
is a Californian kiss,
lunch a felafel with pitta,
tea a lemon pancake.

Whiz around the North Circular,
through the underpass at Edmonton,
change your gears at Palmers Green,
swerve at Southgate.
Drive to me from Romford.

Let's buy a delicatessen smelling of crusty loaves,
brie and olives. We can drink peppermint tea
from brightly coloured mugs,
you can read your weepies.
Please drive to me from Romford.

Stay, paint your toes in turquoise,
with a tint of sapphire highlight.
Wear your flowing flowery dress. We'll go
to the cinema, see something tearful and you can cry,
but don't cry too much.
Come to me from Romford.

Or sparkle along the M25, past lorries and pantechnicons.
Be quick.
Come and read the Sunday papers,
run my bath, share my bath.

We could ride a bus in polished red,
an elephant or kangaroo.
We'll go to Soho,
buy some cakes with layers of cream.
I won't wear my open sandals and on the way back,
through Regent's Park,
we'll feed the ducks — but not fat ones —
and the air will be white wine, crisp with a shot of sun.

I will hold your hand. We'll lie on the grass
and when the band plays you can sing
(and I promise not to)
and if it rains
I'll kiss you dry.
Please drive to me from Romford.

5% PROOF

I love you strong like Ruddles County,
by the pint, straight
down my throat. A frothy fizz
of head, of mellow body,
cool neck, smooth as thigh.

If I were a glass
and you were beer,
I would pour you, feel
you fill me to my lip,
let you settle, just stand
there unsteady, 5% proof,
forever.

GOODNIGHT KISS

A voice of jasmine and stephanotis
whispers in my head,
leads to where I have been before.

The night breeze of her breath,
cool on my face, feels faint.

Her hair frames a sleeping
Essex smile sliding to a grin.

A foot, toes fridge-cold, boots
me, prompting she's there.

Her hand grazes my thigh,
says goodnight.

I lean over, kiss her cheek.

MADNESS

I watch you read, see your eyes
scurry pages, lost in Ireland.
I remember Dublin, our second anniversary.
We drank champagne, a bottle of white wine;
I had a large port to see us to our hotel.

What is it you see in me?
You're not a silly girl,
you tell me that quite often,
but what makes you love me?

Then you undo the buttons on my shirt,
ask me why there are so many.
I laugh when we make love
and you say I'm mad.

LEAP YEAR

It's the 29th of February and my wife
asks if I'll marry her.
'We're already married,' I say.
'Yes,' she says, 'but I'm allowed to ask.'

'But do you still want to,
after all you know about me?
Think hard before you answer.'
'Yes,' she says,
'you've still got that madness in you,
and I've got a lot of work to do.'

REFLECTIONS

i

Sometimes when I trail back my thoughts,
try and find their source,
I just arrive at silence.
Half way there I arrive at a place years gone —
Westgate's beach at high tide,
waves luxuriously dangerous,
flat sand stretching long to the sea,
or the Norfolk Broads,
when I kissed for miles
under cold sky, where spring sun
had no strength to break through.

ii

We are just daydreams.
Some drizzle and others pour like poems,
unforgettable from a haunted place.

Bucket and spade memories
are luminous one moment
then drift away like sand.

iii

The sight of white clematis
hanging level with her eyes,
a poppy planted last year
new and lolling lopsided,
an early rose, its bud
anxious for warmth;
all these are memorable,
but resonate their differences —
sometimes shockingly.

iv

Take an ordinary thing, a dollop
of tomato ketchup shaken from a bottle,
it splats a plate, sprays a restaurant wall,
or a boiled egg cooked till it explodes.
These are photographed, developed,
remembered like a kindness shown
or apology given when none was due.
But where is the first memory of my mother?

v

Grandchildren carry our memories,
or the ones they know.
Tell me about the time . . .
they may say. So I might
be in Portsmouth, near the harbour,
or on the skating rink.
Except I cannot tell of grandfather's Poland.
Maybe a fragment lingers
in an older cousin's mind.

vi

The time is late December
and I think about today and how long
its memory will last.

The sky was shades of white, ribbed
with thinnest cloud, almost transparent
where the burn of sun was strongest.
Wind veered, gusted
and a scurry of birds was swept aside.

Now evening sun has stilled the wind
and the sky lies tired, wrung out.
There is a breeze just cool enough
to chill a darkening blue night.

vii

A horse's head follows me round the corner,
wanders down a childhood street.
His nosebag of everyday brown
hangs from a mouth full of chomp
and jaws grind in slow circles.

I never touched his dirty neck,
far too high to reach.
I could have stroked
a dusty leg, patted the fatness of his belly,
but I always stopped,
and when he moved, shuffled to ease
the boredom, lifted a hoof to mark his spot
or snorted, I ran away.

The horse — I do not know his name
or why his image is so unfaded.
Was it his easy pull-and-tug nature,
outcast face, scruffiness I liked?
I can still hear his harness jangle,
bit frothing in his mouth,
splat of dung, smell its steam,
hear my schoolboy laughter run me home.

I'm going far back, trying to find yesterday.
I don't know how much further I can go.

viii

So when you saw a sparrow flit
across the room, flutter
in the bird bath,
why did I recall a crow, slow
and ambling, dunking itself in a spill of water?

ix

Some memories vanish
others half dissolve,
as notes of music
fluttering into orbit,
return to haunt, evoke
January's darkness,
April's renewal.

I'm looking into the trees,
can hear a sparrow;
now it floats into sight,
loses balance, sways,
flies off, lilting in the distance.

x

The doctor said, 'It's jumped to her chest.'
The antelope in me wheels round,
cannot breathe, freezes,
looks past the moment,
goes a year ahead,
all in half a second.

A dam of tears presses my eyeballs.
I can feel a single drop of wet.
I ask a question, get an answer;
now she's coming in. I'm composed
(outside anyway), stuff a hurried
kleenex in my pocket.
She's here, I smile, get up and we leave.

I can still see the quiver of long grass,
but am more attuned to danger.

xi

I remember my first kiss,
at a party: me skulking on a sofa,
close dancing with a girl who felt
so light in my arms, our kiss,
then the feeling of wanting, being wanted.

Next evening she kissed someone else.
For weeks I couldn't understand.
Now I just think she liked kissing.

xii

Black ghosts swept me into kindergarten.
Those nuns didn't understand a left-handed
Five-year-old who wrote 2 back to front.

Next was posh private, neat uniforms,
peaked cap and red look-at-me blazer.
Here I learnt to spell anxiety.

Siberian Sussex came at nine, sent
on a train shunting from Victoria,
glad to have a strong lock on my tuck box.

At supper we ate bread and dripping,
queued in dressing gowns
for our fix of fat.

I remember the South Downs flooded
with gorse, their burn of yellow flowers,
the bob of rabbits, sound of sea smashing below.

Mother and father came every three weeks.
Lunch at The Grand Brighton: breast of chicken,
chips and mayonnaise — all I would eat,

then a game of table tennis, a handful
of pennies for the West Pier slot machines
and back to school. At night I hugged

my blue bear, felt its face on mine
until I faded into sleep.
Next morning I hid him.

Now I'm right-handed, can write 2
correctly. And Siberia . . .
I've been back. It looks so small.

NIGHT TALES

Sideways rain is falling from a drowsy sky.
It strikes the window in a riot of applause.

Out he goes, my son, up west
for a pizza, a club and the night bus back.

I'll wake when he returns,
hear him quietly close his bedroom door.

He'll sleep till every drop of dance
and beat of music has soaked from his body.

*

The light from the moon
hangs in the window.
In the scrub of darkness
I can see books, towels,
papers, empty wine glasses.

Our bedroom has not been tidied
for two weeks. I don't mind,
it makes me feel like the student
I never was.

'Peter,' my wife says,
'I think we should clear up.'
'Let's leave it a bit longer,' I say,
'I feel younger already.'

*

Tonight was singing its black shadows.
You crept to the bathroom, returned
to find me diagonal across the bed.
You did not wake me,
wanted me to sleep.

You rested at the mattress edge,
enjoyed, you said, my body's heat,
only moved more comfortably
when I snored to the other side.

Morning seeps through the curtains.
You lie still.
Your nightdress is open;
the white of your breast shines in the half light.

*

Morning has its own language;
some thoughts are heavy
as if the day is tired of waking.

But I like remembering when we kissed.
We are sitting on your sofa.
My arm weighs ten stone
when I raise it, place it on your shoulders.

You still say you did not expect it,
but I don't believe you.

*

I'm turned on my side,
one leg out of the covers
to keep half of me cool.

I can hear the gnaw
of a hungry wind
as it chews through the trees.

During the night
I will feel her snuggle into me,
warm the other half.

*

I hear the shriek of foxes,
imagine two bored cubs
starting a squabble.

The night sky has a satin finish,
soft as a Galway accent.
I'm glad I remarried.

*

Tonight I compose a poem in my head,
but let go of its lines
as I lie pillowed in sleep.

I think of my first wife, her death,
how she would have smiled
when my daughter got her first job.

I see her smile,
without the need for words.

*

My head is falling off.
Ex-colleagues are to blame.
It wasn't me who poured
six pints of Stella down my gullet.

My wife pulls off my shoes
lifts my legs onto the bed,
tries to undo my trousers.
I'm enjoying this, but I don't
know how cross she is. I lift
up my bottom and off they come.

'Well Peter,' she says,
'You had a good time.'
'Yes, I have, thank you,' I smile in reply.

'Don't be sick,' I tell myself,
'Just don't be sick.'

LONDON POEMS

RAINBOW OVER THE NORTH CIRCULAR

You straddle the trudge of traffic,
arch your back at the grey crease
of tension, watch it twist with stress
till the yob in all of us, fed up
with being nice, barks back at the wife,
swipes the head of a child, punches
a V sign at another driver.

But you Mr Rainbow,
you with that sideways glance,
lounging over Edmonton and Chingford,
you're taking the piss.
You know your spray of colour,
graffiti in the sky,
will make me smile,
say, 'Look, there's a rainbow.'
But I just don't feel like it.

KING'S ROAD, CHELSEA

This is a street of rocket salad
scattered with flaked parmesan,
where girls and shop windows smile
at each other. Europe is everywhere
and fashion an extravagant egg-and-spoon race.
Bistros buzz their midnight language,
the glitterati spit olive stones, smoke
and talk of closeness to the earth,
natural wealth.

I'm a visitor from the Northern Line,
where a green salad is a starter
not a reproduction Cézanne.
But I could eat King's Road, drink
those white wine Sloanes,
gulp the juice from this place.
I'm on a travel card, a tourist
in the sun. My passport is stamped.
I'm coming back for more.

WEST END GHOSTS

Back in these streets I shiver,
feel ghosts in my bones,
see myself walking towards yesterday,
moves on a monopoly board
through twenty years of bricks and valuations —
dry as mortar.

Oxford Street, Piccadilly, Regent Street.
Here clients crawled in my head, crept
over me. 'No sir, tomorrow is not too soon.
Yes I will sleep standing up
with all your worries in my head.'

Fellow workers of my past speak a jargon
long gone: patter of deals, transactions
with this suit, that briefcase,
names from foreign lands.

Their talk, now my non-language,
floats through my ears; phrases
become lines for poems. I sit and gulp
down beers, plunder the sandwich tray,
try to remember their words,
wary of writing in my notebook.

DH EVANS, OXFORD STREET, W1

Huge coats, coats for women
flapped round burly bodies
flattered by me,
an undeveloped shrimp.
They shimmied and purred,
prowled past mirrors,
big cats, big whiskers.
Coats were my mission,
coats my Saturday job.

I sold camels to the East,
mohair to the rich
and tweed to the gentry.

Rescued by Young Styles,
I had not seen girls
so close before and the more
I saw, the more I smelt
their fresh breath,
no stale lipstick
or powder caked like icing sugar.
This was my place, sniffing
teenage girls; the coats were light,
and I didn't tire.

TRAFALGAR SQUARE

So much yellow, eastern
songs you might say,
swaying time to rhymes
or tears heavy with heat.

Imagine squint of light,
scent of Cyprus,
leaves green with sun.

But here in Trafalgar Square
a lemon grove and yet
is this longing impossible?

I'll plant a hope, a seed
in his, her and your minds.
One morning as scent of lemons blows west
I'll have my wish.

PRIMROSE HILL

Primrose Hill is grandmother:
large body, huge cheeks and the kind
of face that won't let go of life.

Today, standing at the top, below clouds
the colour of grubby underwear,
I see Canary Wharf blink its lights,
bully the East End.

This hill, like a happy memory,
smiles over London. The sky
is clearing to a shade of blue jeans,
faded, ripped at the knees
to let the sun out, warm the air.

Walking home I can't remember
ever sitting on grandmother's lap,
but can still see her hair
tied tight in a bun, her straight back.

SPEAKERS' CORNER

Sometimes I think, 'Why don't I believe?'
It has to do with instinct,
an impulse to doubt.
Point to an oasis in the desert,
I'll tell you it's a mirage.

We're being told to prepare for Hell.
The end is coming;
only God will be our saviour.

Thirsty tourists flood forward,
crowd the watering hole.
Listen, I tell myself,
understand what he's saying.

The man on the soapbox
is getting frenzied.
He seems more frightened
than the fear he's preaching.

I decide not to drink here, move on.

LONDON ZOO

The elephant's legs need a wax,
her swaying face a kiss
and her head a hug.

An Asian lion is snoozing,
the rise and fall of its dusty coat
is a drowsy heartbeat.

A rhino called Rosie shakes
her bottom at me; she's thick-skinned,
not like a poet.

Martin (yes, Martin) the Sumatran tiger
sneers, rolls his eyeballs,
wonders who named him.

The polar bear which stared
and plodded has gone.
I still question if we've got it right or wrong.

TOTTENHAM COURT UNDERGROUND

As I walk to Centre Point
which rears above, encasing
ridges of workers, executives, computers,
I see two curled sleeping bags.

When I return one has made a sign;
it says he's hungry.
Another asks for change.

Sometimes I will give.
But I don't and the words
'Be lucky' follow me down
the ticket concourse,
rattle in my head.

Later, crossing the Heath, I hear
the click of a flick knife opening,
turn to see two foxes
nosing an empty beer can.

WARNER CINEMA VILLAGE, FINCHLEY

The back row of my memory
expects a smoochy place, a mix
of kiss and fumble, steam and passion.
I hear the chatter of crunched popcorn,
slurp and burp of Pepsi, snatches
of last night's sex.

Bars, diners, pizza palaces
they push, make a move on punters.
The Warner is strobe lighting and disco beat,
sweet shop and ice cream parlour.

A toilet sign, pink and slinky, long
and leggy, smiles its come-on.
Here they respect our natural functions.
Do the urinals play the James Bond theme
and the sit-downs the Nutcracker Suite?

Outside, burgers from Wendy's breathe heavy
in my face. The car park chain-smokes,
spews fumes down the lungs of Finchley;
its cough is heard in Southgate.

CAMEL IN CAMDEN TOWN

As I walk to Camden Underground
I think how most camels
are quiet creatures.

A camel parked outside Boots
smiles a long diagonal grin,
tilts his head just enough
to miss a glance of sun on his face.

When I pass, he raises his slow motion neck
stares as if he were a toff
and I a tourist. What
have I done to cause such disdain?

At Burger King kids point
at his knobbly knees and spindly legs.
He crouches and I climb up, hold
the hugeness of his humps,
heat from his body.

As we jollop towards the station
I can feel his quietness, want his calm.

THEATRE LAND

Here I saw Rattigan's Separate Tables,
stiff white tablecloths,
neat knives and forks
reflecting a shade of Englishness.

Not a country garden with close-cut
lawn and borders unrestrained with colour,
or a drunken belly hung over tight trousers,

but the part of me that feels
like a starched tablecloth,
ironed out flat, the odd stain
hidden by salt and pepper pots.

Theatre is a poem working.
When I hear its voice
hard behind my eyes,
then I see truth, hold faith.

Drury Lane, Strand, Shaftesbury Avenue.

BIG BEN

My school friend was called Ben,
Peter Ben. He was big, good at Maths,
played his calculator like a piano,
with two hands, always came top.

As I stare at this clock,
its straight back facing Parliament
where many have tried to strike a difference,
I think about now, my past,
how my children will remember me.

It's the time we give that chimes loudest.
I look at the clock, see it's getting late.

BRICK LANE, E1

Too young to feel the blackshirt shadow,
kick of its silhouette;
but I heard the tongue of the BNP
and felt my forehead sweat.

REGENT'S CANAL

Yellow sun and blue sky have greened
the canal to dusty emerald.
A barge sweeps past, swamping
crisp packets, its chug chug
soothing me. But where is the horse?
No clipitty-clop on the towpath
or pull and plod of its doleful stare?

I'm a walker, reluctant, till promised
a beer in The Engineer. A cold Grolsch
gushes, ribbons down, revives my feet.

Setting sun has muddied the canal
to brown. Under a bridge I hear
the whinny of a horse,
spot it disappearing into dusk.

LONDON COUSINS

Sometimes I worry about Hampstead:
streets peppered with restaurants,
boutiques fighting for frontage,
Melvyn Bragg combing his hair.

Camden looks shiftily over his shoulder,
still the scruffy hooligan,
gets togged up at weekends.

St John's Wood thinks she's Beverly Hills,
sways her hips, wears
designer burglar alarms.

Kilburn sprawls his lanky High Road,
has a tendency to oversleep,
turns his back on Maida Vale;
she's a social climber —
sexpot made good.

Swiss Cottage is a bit mixed up,
feels anxious, and Finchley
(a second cousin) is doing better;
Waitrose has opened,
there's a Warner Cinema.

I begin to understand
why cousins grow apart.

FOX TALES

FOREST FOX

He sensed my hesitation, untangled
my thoughts, disappeared before the sound
of heartbeat crossed the clearing.
Why do foxes think they're God's gift?

I followed, felt the ground give, squelch
of boots in mud and moss, heard the crack
of twigs as I plodded after him. He scampered
away, called me on, barked my name.

The rain came so cold it scorched
my cheeks and still the fox howled onwards,
turned his head towards me as he fox-trotted
through the fist of the forest.

On till gloom became darkness. We stopped.
He faced me. His drowned eyes stared
as he nosed the air; his coat was frost,
his mouth spit and steam.

I crouched to within a sniff of his face,
dared to ask, 'Do you believe . . .
and who will remember you when you die?'
'It's not about belief,' he said.

I reached and touched his head, felt slicked down
crisp fur, saw that fox as I would never
again; then he licked me, turned, bounded off,
faded into the thick of morning mist.

KITCHEN FOX

There it was, a vixen (I think),
sitting on the table, rather sultry;
her curved back groomed
for an evening out.

We spotted each other and concrete
weighted my feet. Her sun eyes
stared, didn't blink.
Her whiskers twitched.

Who would move first? Not me.
She was tall and slinky.
Her cheeks were shallow
with white mouth, slightly dirty.

Anyway, I couldn't move—was stuck
to the kitchen floor.
Her tail lay broad and silent.
Then I heard a gush, saw

the table flood with fox piss.
It spilt over to my feet
and when I looked up she'd gone—
out through the kitchen door

and I still couldn't move.

HEATHLAND FOX

The sky was forged with metal light,
stuttered its confessions over the heath,

and when it rained, hard bullet rain,
the fox appeared, crossed in front of me,

swaggered out of the scrub beside a ditch.
I felt as if I'd just been kissed;

his russet coat moved in symmetrical equations
as shoulders and haunches strode into the gloom.

Everything was fox: serrated grin,
panting tongue, the confidence of a toff,

and yet, as he turned into the watery shadows
I noticed his eyes were a different disposition.

His backwards glance did it.
You can tell by the eyes.

DESERT FOX

It's Israel and the sky
has been washed
from blue to apricot.

Our coach cuts the desert
and in front is a fox
caught in the surprise of our lights.

Giddy from the day's sun,
head hung low,
he edges from the hem of the sand.

His back carries the weight
of years of heat
baked into his coat.

I envy the thought of his anger,
how he won't let go
of his toasted crust of ground.

He sits and licks his feet,
a long slow tongue,
soothing away the sting.

Our driver honks his horn
and in a flash of fox
the road is empty.

POEMS HAVE NO STAMINA

FRAILTY

What is it about frailty
that makes me want to cry?
I see a boisterous silence,
a stutter of reason,
thoughts arising out of near madness.
I hear my heart say, 'Yes, this I know,'
and empathy becomes reality.

So now we both are swinging
on the same curve of experience
and for a short shared moment
I am you, part of your past
and feel both our tears.

HEALING

You ask me about healing.
Go and see the place where your
deckchair
rests in shade, under the plum.
Look at the trodden track
towards that scrap of dry ground,
then remember spring.

Imagine a cluster of snowdrops
their white buds in new grass.
This is renewal, not prayer;
it should happen naturally
but often needs some help.

MOOD

When I close my eyes, not tight
but as slatted shutters,
— the kind found on a Cotswold house
which lets sun and past glimpse in —
I hear memories, see snowstorms
that taste of sugar and childhood.

If I slam my eyes shut,
pillow my head deep inside myself,
it's as if that past falls away
and light turns to bitten nails.

I suppose we call it mood.
It's best if our eyes stay open.
Don't ask me why,
it's just better that way.

UNDER BRIDGES

It is always a frightening thought,
but floating, eyes closed
there's a trembling.

The rowboat drifts between time
and bridges. Morning sun
strikes afternoon
and I open my eyes.
The bridges still come, flow past.

WOMEN

Face, body, hands; watch the way
they flick their hair over a bare ear.
Heart is important;
go for the biggest available.
So is heat: sizzling skin,
a hot soul and breath the taste
of chablis, smell of raspberries.
Cold noses are difficult to warm
but it's worth the effort.
Voice is up there; loud
causes fright; too soft and you drift away.
Never go for money,
don't go for social standing
your habits will embarrass her.
Find a woman with common sense,
some of it may rub off.
If you care, so will she.
Never borrow her bicycle;
always eat her apple cake
and if you have a row
maintain foot contact in bed.

CHUTZPAH

Buildings bulge with testosterone,
square shoulders, big hips,
strut the streets, edge for skyline,
a pinnacle, a career.

Unlanguaged cab drivers
pothole me, screech brakes,
pound horns. Here, greed
is a byword and nerd a no-go.
Fresh means a pastrami on rye,
thick sliced, plenty mustard
and a double decaf is hell hot,
and tastes of Colombia.

In this city a kiss is not full on,
it's a kiss into air: 'You son of a bitch,
why don't you look where I'm going?'
Here a fabulous figure is the bottom line,
a relationship is lunch,
and romance a Disney film.

This is where the greenback stamps
his feet, acts the spoilt child.
Here lipstick has a permanent gloss
and neon flashes chutzpah.

SHADES OF GREEN

I hear them as day climbs out of the sky
in the low wind before the sun has risen—
the first sounds of morning,
a trill from a sparrow eager for love,
drone of a melancholy pigeon,
the birth of shades of green.

Some are almost yellow, others the hue
of young grass, limes, olives, avocados.
And scattered in between is khaki, emerald,
the blue-green of ageing pine, years of birdsong
on hillsides and heaths.

Some say the first song of day comes from within,
a sigh when we wake, touch of a hand.
I'm not sure.
Listen to those early morning songs,
look at all that green.

NIGHT WATCH

As I look into the sky
I see a string of stars,
or are they poets, clustered
to blaze more brilliantly?

Tonight the moon is as close
as I have ever seen it.
Hanging like a white peach,
it lights the night air
and in soaring darkness
between the glare of stars
is space, bare and blacker
than any ocean or chasm.

Do I believe
in the wisdom of stars?

I reach out, stretch higher
until they are within a glimmer.
It's late and in the cold distance
I can see a pinch of sun.

It slowly burns to a glow
and as it does, the stars vanish.

THE ANTI-SICKNESS DREAM

He shook my hand with his left,
the right stump withered,
tucked under.

I wondered.
I admired his guts,
his presence. I patronized.

Lucky he could walk on his feet.
No need to swing on knuckles.
He had a desk,
wore a three-piece
and an intellect
not bitter, not jealous.

His mother had reached
for that fruit,
the anti-sickness dream.
At birth she was crushed.

She now swings on her knuckles.
He walks high,
bears no grudge?

ENGLISHMAN IN PALM BEACH

I'm in shorts, M&S new season specials;
they fit my weight
but I still look a scruff.
Maybe it's the baseball cap,
But I don't belong in this street.

Here skin is stretched tight as parchment,
tucked under bony chins,
behind aged ears. Noses are small,
chipped into shape. Am I tempted?
Sure. But I like my rugged looks;
a dinky nose is not my personality.

We stop for a sandwich. What I want
is egg and Heinz salad cream, a taste
of England. But I get a symphony of lettuce,
tomatoes sliced the size of cartwheels,
olives, and in the centre, blocking
out the sun, bulging egg and mayo,
is my sandwich. It shouts
eat me, eat me, and I do.

Outside we trample an anorexic Floridian.
She's being walked by poodles Chloe and Joey.
They've had face jobs and look like . . . dogs.
I apologise. My English accent rescues me.
'I love your accent,' she says.
'I love yours too,' I reply, and follow Janine,

my all-American sister-in-law, into the glow
of the street. We pass Saks, Emanuel Ungaro
towards Chanel. She needs the restroom —
toilet to you and me. This store has clean toilets.
Here you could have a medical intervention
on the floor. 'Janine,' I say, 'you can't
just use the toilet, not buy anything.'
'Come with me,' she says.
But I can't. She strides off, cool as cream.

As we drive away, the sun beams over Palm Beach.
I cross my legs.

KISSING INTO AIR

A kiss on the cheeks would be too easy.
The air kiss, off the side of the face,
in front of the lower ear,
that's more difficult, designed for experts,
not drunk or tipsy poets.

What are the rules? Don't touch cheeks,
and if you do, just the lightest accidental
scuff of skin. Not enough
to smell perfume, shampoo or lipstick,
but close enough to blow your kiss past her head,
out into the foreign land where kisses go —
a wasted kiss, a kiss no good to anyone.
Mwah, mwah.

WINTER JOINTS

Warm towels on my stomach,
knees under my chest,
arms flung across the room.
I'm sideways on the table edge,
tilted under his smile,
I think I'll fall off
but I won't get past those hands.

He wants to go clickabout.
Is he asking or telling?
This is not for a half-cured hypochondriac.

He's decided my head's not with him,
realises I can't make decisions.
I'm trapped in my underpants
and he still talks anatomy,
holds up a skeleton.
Was it a patient?

Now he's pummelling.
I feel his weight.
Heavy, light, heavy . . .
click to the right,
click to the left.

'How do you feel?' he asks.
'I think I've done quite well,' I say
and can't help laughing.
'Yes, but I've had all the fun,' he says.

I bend to tie my laces,
feel the joint twinge.

FRENCH RIVIERA

'Bonjour, comment allez-vous?'
This sea is so French,
wears a classic chic dress,
ripples, shimmies in light turquoise
sweeping low-backed to the beach.

She laps my feet, nibbles at my toes,
whispers soft foam as I step ankle-high
in warm slush of her wash.

Now I'm in the swim of her arms
submerged in waves, just floating
in a weightless caress, treading breath.

HILLS AT INVERGARRY

The hills at Invergarry lean
into the loch, silent, well-mannered.
When height was everything
they longed to be mountains,
compete with Ben Nevis.

Life could have been huge vistas,
cable cars, flashing lights, News at Ten.
Now rounded backs reflect in the loch
glad their peaks don't reach the coldest clouds.

Brushed by fading light
the hills relax into their glens,
sip at Loch Oich,
enjoy an evening dram.

SEPTEMBER WIND

Winter wind has come early,
thrashes about, seems
to have lost its way.

The trees argue, stand
up for themselves, try
to hold on to their leaves.

Sun melts through the sky,
warms an inside-out day
and that's how I feel,
a bit inside-out. How strange.

WORDS

When wind is on the hunt,
a thug out for a fight,
a fist of knuckle beats
rain from the sky.
Clouds lie shaken, empty.

Sometimes, words will blow up,
pounce, knock us to the ground
and the violence of what we hear
dries out our tears,
leaves a storm of silence.

FRAYED AT THE EDGES

Hypochondria
is a cowardly vulture.
It circles and swoops
on weakened prey,
no frontal attack or charge
to rip my body apart. Just
a tug, tug, tugging, tormenting
the tissue of my mind
to grind me down. Debilitated.

Not too debilitated to discover
lumps in my armpits,
tumours in my brain and groin,
lymph nodes erupting,
malignancy everywhere—but nowhere.

But the uncontrollable can be tamed,
the funeral black vulture subdued
and fear dulled.

So I try not to think
(that would be too silly)
that three out of four
will become seriously ill,
and the chances are—
I probably will.

THE OLD JEWISH CEMETERY, PRAGUE
(closed 1787)

Stacked deep,
twenty thousand bodies
lie beneath tombstones
shaped like chipped decayed teeth.

They heard jackboots
stomp, cattle trucks
shunt to clear the ghettos,
pack the camps.

They saw the threat
from the hammer and sickle,
tanks rumble, bludgeon.
Crush.

They smelt scorched
skin from Wenceslas Square,
heard the striking students
and euphoria of freedom.

Now coaches disgorge
tourists who snake and jabber past.
The peace of twenty thousand
is disturbed again.

COWS

I've been thinking about cows,
the sort we see in a lush of grass,
lummoxing about
as we speed past in a train,
our faces pressed to a misty window.

I love the way they don't seem to
worry about tomorrow, how
their runny noses
cause no disdain to each other,
how they wobble when they stand up
and flop down like graceless aunts
when they're tired.

I want to get close to a cow,
close enough to hear the snort of its breath,
see the dark moon of its eyes.
I want to pat the broad field
of its head and say thank you
for all that milk, butter and cheese.

THE LAKES

In the hills I'm level with treetops.
I know what they search for —
their highest branches and leaves
try to glimpse where our spirits go.
But the veil of mist
does not reveal those secrets.

Down in the valley, there is a silver gloss
over the lake, and on a green verge
sheep are chewing gourmet grass.

Years ago I sipped from every spring I found,
had never seen cold water gush
straight from the ground, splashed
my cheeks, drank so much
I went psychedelic.

I can hear the groan of waterfalls,
sound of stories from streams,
purr of poems from rivers.
Thin rain is the past on my face.
I lick my lips, taste a soft memory.

POEMS HAVE NO STAMINA

I wait for the first breath of a poem,
the light touch inside my head
which builds to a burst of pressure,
then pours a scurry of words
to write itself, almost whole.

Most poems don't start with a breath.
They splutter, make a nuisance
of themselves, lounge around
on the sofa, not neatly upright,
but lying out full-length, shoes on.

'Please get up,' I say.
'Come out where I can hear you.'
They are shy or awkward or both.
I try to be friendly.
'All I want to do is write you down,
see your words, listen to your voice.'

In time, if I appear not to care,
am not too eager, a second line
will follow the first, then a stanza.

But poems have no stamina,
become fractious, need cajoling.
'Don't sod me about,' I say.
'Be good, behave.
Now that wasn't too much trouble, was it?'

For a list of Hearing Eye
publications, please write
enclosing an SAE to:

Hearing Eye,
Box 1,
99 Torriano Avenue,
London
NW5 2RX

Alternatively, visit the
Hearing Eye website at:

http://www.torriano.org